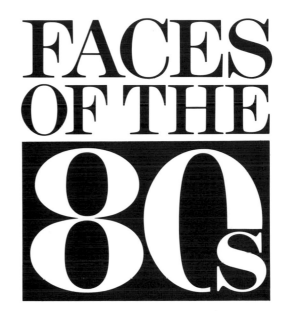

FACES OF THE 80s

GEMMA LEVINE'S

FACES OF THE 8Os

TEXT BY
JEFFREY ARCHER,
HUMPHRY BERKELEY,
AND OTHERS

FOREWORD BY THE RT HON
MARGARET THATCHER
FRS MP

IN AID OF THE SHARON ALLEN LEUKAEMIA TRUST

FOR MAE and ELLIS
(My parents)

First Publication in Great Britain

First Published in 1987 by Collins Publishers
8 Grafton St, London W1X 3LA

Photographs © Gemma Levine
Design and compilation © BLA Publishing Limited
East Grinstead, Sussex, England
A member of the **Ling Kee Group**
LONDON · HONG KONG · TAIPEI · SINGAPORE · NEW YORK

Printed in Spain by Heraclio Fournier SA

— HER ROYAL HIGHNESS PRINCESS MICHAEL OF KENT —

Patron of the Sharon Allen Leukaemia Trust

1O DOWNING STREET

LONDON SW1A 2AA

THE PRIME MINISTER

    The Sharon Allen Leukaemia Trust works to care for those who suffer from one of the most distressing of all human illnesses. In the short time since it was formed in 1984 it has made a significant contribution by providing extra funds for equipment to treat leukaemia patients.

    The need for such treatment and care is sad and sometimes tragic. But it is heartening to know of the endeavours of such voluntary organisations in support of our NHS facilities.

    All royalties from the sales of this book will go to the Sharon Allen Leukaemia Trust to help it continue and expand its important work. I wish the Trust most sincere good wishes for the future; and thank all who contribute to that future by buying this excellent book.

Margaret Thatcher

JULY 1987

THE RT HON MARGARET THATCHER

ACKNOWLEDGEMENTS

I would like to express my personal gratitude to the following sponsors. Without their generous support the exhibition, or this publication could not have materialised.

The Hillsdown Charitable Trust
The Dixons Group Charitable Trust
Mr Jarvis Astaire
Mr Trevor Chinn
Dr Davide Sala
Kodak plc
The Ronson Foundation
The Bernard Sunley Charitable Foundation
The Contship Group

My thanks to Gordon Bishop Associates, my black and white printers, who worked with me in great haste through the year.

Susan Bradman, who has given her time generously to alert the media and her time to being my friend.

Candida, for rendering endless cups of coffee to over two hundred and fifty sitters.

Mrs Jane Russell, who has tirelessly and with great humour assisted with the diary.

Mr Simon Friend whose collaboration was invaluable.

A special mention, with fond thanks, to Lady Falkender, whose inspiration it was to join me, together with SALT, to create 'Faces of the 80s'.

GEMMA LEVINE
November 1987

INTRODUCTION

On behalf of the Trustees and Honorary Officers of the Sharon Allen Leukaemia Trust, I would like to express our gratitude and thanks to Gemma Levine for her brilliant photographs and also for giving this charity a year of her life.

It goes without saying that we are immensely grateful to the Prime Minister for writing an introduction to the book, to Jeffrey Archer for his text, to Simon Blacker for designing the book and to Collins, for publishing it.

We, naturally, wish to thank everyone who was kind enough to spare the time to be photographed and, in particular, all our sponsors without whose generous help the exhibition FACES OF THE 80s and this book would not have got off the ground.

The Sharon Allen Leukaemia Trust, known as SALT, is a medical charity which was founded in 1984 to raise money to provide care and treatment for leukaemia sufferers when their needs cannot be met by the National Health Service. Leukaemia is the single biggest killer of children after road accidents; over half those who get this disease are children between the ages of two and twelve. SALT is named after Sharon Allen, a little girl of nine, who has leukaemia.

Our major commitment is to Westminster Hospital. We are committed to give this hospital £100 000 to buy much needed expensive new equipment, and we are paying the salary of a member of its medical staff who is responsible for co ordinating its bone marrow transplant programme. We are anxious to continue and increase this particular commitment and also to increase our help to NHS hospitals outside London.

All the royalties from this book will go to SALT and if anyone would like to make an additional contribution to our work they can do so by sending a donation to the Sharon Allen Leukaemia Trust, FREEPOST, London SW1X 0BR.

HUMPHRY BERKELEY
Director

ALED JONES

Aled Jones was discovered singing in a church choir in his native Anglesey and subsequently became the subject of a touching BBC TV documentary. Since then the unearthly beauty and purity of his treble voice has delighted millions, in a repertory ranging from Handel to Lloyd Webber, Bach to Bernstein. His biggest hit, however, was the catchy theme-tune to the cartoon film of Raymond Briggs' The Snowman. Since his retirement from his juvenile singing career, Aled has proved a charming and confident chat-show host. Will he re-emerge as a great opera singer of the 1990s? Everyone must hope so.

GWEN FFRANGCON-DAVIES

Gwen Ffrangcon-Davies is ninety-six and has had a presence on the English stage for the last sixty-five years. A Shakespearean actress of note, her first London success was in *The Immortal Hour* in 1922 and she created the part of Eve in Shaw's *Back to Methuselah*. She has been in numerous radio and TV plays, and enjoys gardening.

JEFFREY ARCHER

Jeffrey Archer's career has been more sensational than any of his novels. In 1969, aged twenty-nine, he was the youngest MP and became a millionaire. Five years later, he was facing bankruptcy, and resigned from Parliament. His first novel, *Not a Penny More, Not a Penny Less*, was followed by many others and he is now one of the most widely read novelists in the world. He returned to politics in 1985 as Deputy Chairman of the Conservative Party and resigned fourteen months later after a paper claimed he had had an involvement with a call girl. He made legal history in his libel case against *The Star* by being awarded half a million pounds in damages, the largest amount ever to have been awarded in a British libel case. Politics are his abiding passion. Will he return? With Jeffrey everything is possible. (contributed by Humphry Berkeley)

JOAN COLLINS

Joan Collins is an actress, a writer and the mother of three children—although most people think of her as Alexis in *Dynasty*. She actively supports several charities that deal with the handicapped and is one of the most successful television actresses in the world. She has been an actress for over thirty years and has become the role model for the woman over forty, proving that one can still be attractive and desirable. A leader of fashion she is considered to be one of the most glamorous women in Europe.

TESSA SANDERSON

Tessa Sanderson won a gold medal at the Los Angeles Olympics in 1984. She and Fatima Whitbread have dominated world javelin throwing during the eighties, and undoubtedly will be the leading contenders for the Seoul Olympics of 1988. Miss Sanderson was awarded an MBE in 1985 for her services to athletics, and hopes to become a presenter of children's programmes when she retires.

BEN KINGSLEY

Born in Manchester of Indian parentage, Ben Kingsley first established himself as a star of the Royal Shakespeare Company, for whom he played Hamlet, Ariel in *The Tempest*, among many other challenging roles. Then, in 1980, he played Mahatma Gandhi in Sir Richard Attenborough's film about the great Indian leader, for which he won a clutch of major awards, including the Oscar for Best Actor. Since then he has returned to the Royal Shakespeare Company as Othello and played the great nineteenth-century actor Edmund Kean in a one-man show.

PATRICK STEPTOE

One of the foremost names in one of the most controversial and experimental areas of medicine is Patrick Steptoe. He was director of the Oldham Centre for Human Reproduction, from 1969 to 1979, before starting work on the development of 'test-tube' babies. One of his recent successes was with frozen twin foetuses—one child being born a year after the other. Dr Steptoe is also a keen connoisseur of wine, and in 1985 he became a Commandant of the Tastevin de Bourgogne.

TONY WHITEHEAD

In 1983 Tony Whitehead, previously a worker in health education, became the first director of the Terrence Higgins Trust, a charitable organization dedicated to the fight against the 'at present' incurable disease of AIDS. As AIDS has spread, so has the Trust's work—both in terms of personnel (over a thousand volunteers and ten full-time staff) and the money it receives (over £1½ million a year at the last count). The Trust both educates the public in the facts about AIDS and counsels and supports people with the disease.

GENERAL EVA BURROWS

As tough and hard-working as she is kindly and sympathetic, the remarkable Eva Burrows continues the great traditions of the Salvation Army, of which she was appointed General in 1986. Her colourful and exciting career with the Army took her from her native Australia to Zimbabwe (then Rhodesia), where she spent fifteen years, and then to Sri Lanka. Dedicated to putting the Christian faith and virtues into action, Eva Burrows is leading the Salvation Army towards the twenty-first century and the challenge of a new set of social problems.

SIR ROY STRONG

Sir Roy Strong is a larger than life character. He has recently retired after being Director of the Victoria and Albert Museum since 1974. He is married and, amongst many other things, enjoys gardening, cooking and country life. He is also a writer and his latest book is *Gloriana: Portraits of Queen Elizabeth I.*

BOB GELDOF

Bob Geldof captured the imagination of the whole world with his *Live Aid* concert to raise money for the starving in Ethiopia—a concert that raised £50 million, with another £8 million added from the sales of the recordings of *Do You Know It's Christmas?* Single-handed, he probably did more than any politician to bring the plight of the Third World into perspective, while at the same time proving, as all our children can testify, how much the young care.

RICHARD BRANSON

Richard Branson is a 'modern Brit' very much in the character of Francis Drake and Captain Morgan. I suspect that, had he been born in the seventeenth century, he would have been a pirate, but would have given most of his spoils to the Queen. Balloonist, yachtsman and Chairman of Virgin Records should be enough for one man, but he has recently added the chairmanship of the environmental group UK 2000, a £23-million government campaign to clean up Britain.

MICHAEL GRADE

Michael Grade is a genuine entrepreneur, which makes it all the more surprising that the BBC employed him as head of programmes. Whichever team he plays for, his only interest is to see that it wins. As he sits behind his vast desk at BBC headquarters tugging at his braces, one can hear him saying, 'Never mind the quality—just look at the ratings'. Underneath the self-inflicted image is the man most likely to dominate television in the nineties. He is the son of Leslie Grade, the theatrical agent, and nephew of Lord Grade and Bernie Delfont.

ANNE DIAMOND

Anne Diamond's easy-going manner and casual interviewing on TV AM belie a tough and highly professional journalist. Often the seemingly innocent question catches politicians and film stars alike off guard, leaving them with headlines that they live to regret. Other women television personalities have come and gone during the decade. I suspect Miss Diamond is here to stay.

SIR ALASTAIR BURNET

Sir Alastair Burnet, one of Britain's most distinguished and respected journalists, has during the eighties become one of the most familiar faces on television. He is probably best known as the front man on *News at Ten*, but it is his work as editor of a national newspaper and his professionalism as anchor man for ITV during the election campaign that have set standards which have made coverage of politics in Britain the envy of the television world.

SIR PETER PARKER

Sir Peter Parker will probably be best remembered for his revitalization of British Rail, of which he was Chairman from 1971 to 1983. Many of the improvements that we now take for granted might never have come about without Sir Peter's tenacity and vision. He is now Chairman of the Rockware Group and a keen amateur sportsman, who once played rugby for Bedford and East Midlands.

GERALDINE JAMES

Generally acclaimed as the finest serial ever made for British television, Granada TV's adaptation of Paul Scott's novels 'The Raj Quartet' as *The Jewel in the Crown* brought many new talents to the public's attention—not least that of Geraldine James, who movingly played the role of Sarah Leyton. Recently she has proved herself an accomplished comedienne, both on television (*Blott on the Landscape*) and in the West End (*When I was a Girl I Used to Sing and Shout*).

LIZZIE WEBB

Lizzie Webb was a teacher of English dancing at a boys school in London, some of whom were skin heads. For a year she taught the mentally handicapped in a school for disturbed adolescents. She was 'discovered' by one of her keep-fit pupils and became the early morning TV keep-fit girl. She now does a lot of writing for children and has made a gold winning video. Her exercises are worthy of an acrobat. She looks a mere girl but is in fact an incredible thirty-nine.

ARTHUR SCARGILL

Arthur Scargill is President of the National Union of Mineworkers. He is the bogey man of the Left used, he suspects, by Conservative canvassers to persuade people not to vote Liberal for fear of a Labour government dominated by him. He is mild mannered and courteous to meet. His rabble rousing is reserved for rallies and media events.

LORD SIEFF

Lord Sieff was until 1985 President of Marks and Spencer. He has served his country both as a colonel in the Royal Artillery during the last war, and as a member of the House of Lords where he currently sits. In his early life he played a major role in the founding of the modern state of Israel, and he has been used by several prime ministers as a go-between whenever there has been a crisis in that country. But his proudest boast is that most of the goods sold in Marks and Spencer are British made. At seventy-four he remains a director of several companies, but he spends more time administering his charitable trust than the day-to-day running of any of the companies he has been responsible for building.

LORD KING OF WARTNABY

Lord King is the dynamic Chairman of British Airways. As a true son of Leicestershire, he was Master of Foxhounds of Badsworth and the Duke of Rutland's Foxhounds (Belvoir) and Chairman of the Belvoir Hunt. He expects to get his own way and is surprised when he does not.

HARRY SOLOMON

Harry Solomon, the charismatic Chairman of Hillsdown Holdings, was a qualified solicitor and practised for many years. He sponsors the London International Opera Festival and has a great love of music and the theatre. He jogs, enjoys cricket and has an active social life.

SIR IMMANUEL JAKOBOVITS

To anyone outside the Jewish religion, the word 'Rabbi' may conjure up the image of a venerable old gentleman devoting himself to the scriptures. But Chief Rabbi of the United Hebrew Congregations of the British Commonwealth of Nations Sir Immanuel Jakobovits is someone very much in touch with the great social and political problems facing the world today.

CARDINAL BASIL HUME

Cardinal Hume, Archbishop of Westminster, is the first Catholic Archbishop to become a major national figure since Cardinal Manning, and he is the first Archbishop of Westminster to have been a monk. Now that the tradition of an Italian Pope has been broken so successfully by Pope John Paul II, Cardinal Hume might be regarded as a favourite to become the second English Pope. To those who know him, what is instantly recognizable is his quality of holiness.

SIR SIGMUND STERNBERG

Budapest-born Sir Sigmund has been Chairman of the Commodities Research Unit Holdings since 1983. He has involved himself in many organizations concerned to foster better relations and understanding between the Jewish and Christian communities in this country. He is also a JP.

LORD LANE

Held in respect by all who come in contact with him, Geoffrey Dawson Lane has been Lord Chief Justice of England since the beginning of the decade, having been appointed a judge in 1966. Educated at Shrewsbury and Trinity College, Cambridge (of which he was made an honorary fellow in 1981), Lord Lane served in the RAF throughout the Second World War and was called to the Bar in 1946. In the many cases in which he has had to advise, Lord Lane has embodied the qualities for which British justice and common sense are so respected in the world.

PAUL HAMLYN

Paul Hamlyn has the distinction of having created two publishing empires in one lifetime and made his fortune through each of them. His donations to charity are legendary. He is an opera and ballet addict and is the creator of *Paul Hamlyn Week* at the Royal Opera House, Covent Garden, which allows people who have never been to the Opera House to buy tickets at £2 each.

BERNARD LEVIN

Arguably the leading columnist in Great Britain today, Mr Levin can write authoritatively on everything from opera to road walking in Tuscany, but perhaps it is his sharp political insights that have made his columns in *The Times* required reading for every member of the Houses of Parliament. A man who will rank with Neville Cardus and Alastair Cooke as one of the three most versatile writers of their age.

MIKE GATTING

Mike Gatting had the unenviable task of taking over the captaincy of Middlesex and England from Mike Brearley. Modern captains seem to come in for nothing but criticism, though Gatting has stuck steadfastly to the task of leading his country. He has led his county (Middlesex) to victory in the County Championship table, and England to an Ashes win in Australia.

FRANK BRUNO

Frank Bruno began his distinguished boxing career by winning the WBA amateur championship at the age of eighteen. Soon after this he turned professional, winning twenty-seven of his twenty-nine professional bouts. He lost only to Tim Witherspoon, a former world champion, and 'Bonecrusher' Smith. Frank Bruno has looked our best chance of gaining a world championship since Henry Cooper knocked down Mohamed Ali, and he could still make it in the eighties.

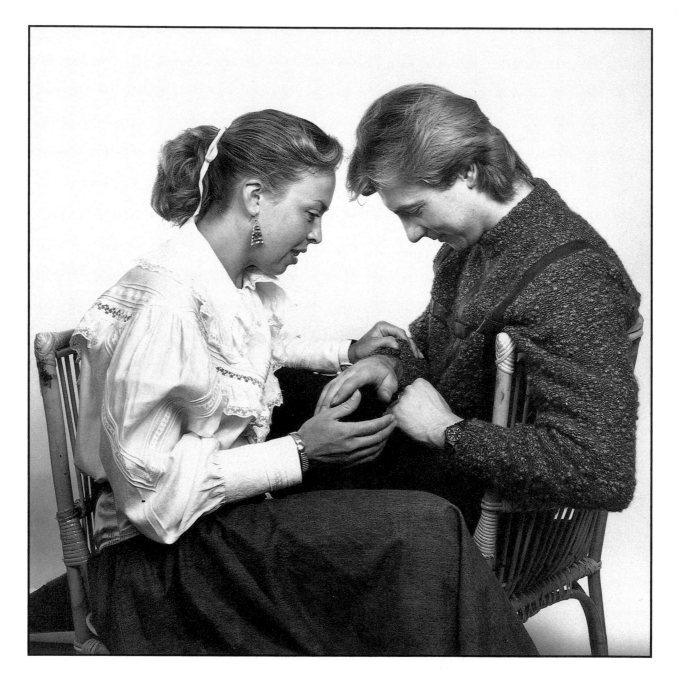

JAYNE TORVILL AND CHRISTOPHER DEAN

Jayne Torvill and Christopher Dean, the Fonteyn and Nureyev of the ice rink, became partners in 1975 while Christopher was a policeman, They started winning championships in 1981, and have never looked back. 1984 was a spectacular year and one to remember. They won the gold medal at the European Championship, at the Olympic Games, and at the World Championship. Their first tour of Australia and New Zealand broke all box-office records and *The Song of India* was unveiled at the Royal Command Performance by satellite from Australia. Sadly, they might have reached their peak in the eighties, but what a peak!

THE EMMANUELS

Seven hundred million eyes of TV viewers were on the dress which this talented couple created for Lady Diana Spencer when she married the Prince of Wales in 1981. They continue to design some of her clothes and also appeared with the Princess in a BBC documentary *In Private—In Public*.

STANLEY KALMS

Stanley Kalms is the founder and Chairman of the dynamic Dixon Group and has spent his whole career with the Group. He started in 1948 in the one store owned by his father, before going public fourteen years later when he was still only thirty-one. His is one of the great success stories of the era.

MICHAEL HESELTINE

One of the most charismatic figures of the decade, Mr Heseltine resigned as Secretary of State for Defence during the Westland crisis of 1986. After his term as President of the Oxford Union there was never any doubt he would want to enter the House of Commons, and when he did enter the House of Commons there was never any doubt that he would hold high office. He served in the governments of Edward Heath and Margaret Thatcher and, unlike most resigning ministers, has remained a full-time active politician with only one unfulfilled ambition for the nineties.

JOLEY RICHARDSON

Joley Richardson, the granddaughter of Sir Michael Redgrave and daughter of Tony Richardson and Vanessa Redgrave, comes from one of our greatest theatrical families. She has played Helena in *A Midsummer Night's Dream* and the third witch in *Macbeth* for the Royal Shakespeare Company. She was Dominique in BBC Television's *Body Contact*. Those who know her believe that she will be as great an actress as her mother.

THE EARL OF LONGFORD

Frank Longford held many ministerial posts in various Labour governments, both under Attlee and Wilson. He started life as a Conservative and was converted by his wife, Elizabeth, to Socialism. She started life as an atheist and was converted by him to Catholicism. Most of his time is now spent on prison visiting and prison reform. He is most recognizable by the back of his head, which is unique and unmistakable.

THE ROUX BROTHERS

Reviving the old traditions of dining-out in the grand style, with lavish food and superb service, the Roux brothers are two of the country's leading chefs and restaurateurs. Michael Roux is based at the beautiful Waterside Inn at Bray in Berkshire, and his brother Albert can be found at Le Gavroche in London's Belgravia. They have also written a highly successful and sophisticated cookery book, *New Classic Cuisine*.

PRUE LEITH

Prue Leith spent her childhood in South Africa. She started cooking boardroom lunches from her London bedsitter in 1960. This blossomed into Leith's Good Food Commercial Catering, Leith's Restaurant, Leith's School of Food and Wine and Leith's Farm. She has grown from the girl who cooked lunches for directors in boardrooms into one of the greatest experts in *grande cuisine* in the country. Her own tastes are simple and her favourite meal is scrambled eggs. She once acted as a chef for a day with British Rail to show that meals on trains need not be so dull.

SIR ROBIN DAY

The political face of the eighties, probably as well known as any prime minister. His sharp, tough questioning has made him the interviewer most politicians dread to face. All those who spend their life in politics realize that he would have made a splendid Cabinet minister himself, if only he could have found one party he could continually have agreed with. He and Frank Muir have kept the bow-tie industry in business single-handed.

DAVID PUTTNAM

One of those rare Englishmen who have dominated the film world. He is currently chief executive of Columbia Pictures, but he is probably best remembered for the two Oscar-winning films, *Chariots of Fire* and *The Killing Fields*. He is currently a director of Anglia Television, a trustee of the Tate Gallery and a supporter of Tottenham Hotspur FC.

SIR DAVID NAPLEY

Sir David Napley is probably one of England's most expensive and successful solicitors. He defended Jeremy Thorpe and Harvey Proctor. Anyone in a jam should go to him for advice. He looks like a medieval Italian Cardinal, but in every other respect he is very much a man of the eighties.

JEREMY IRONS

When Evelyn Waugh's romantic novel *Brideshead Revisited* was adapted for television by Granada TV in 1981, Jeremy Irons became overnight a household name. His portrayal of the laconic Charles Ryder and his doomed relationships with the tragic Marchmain family has since been seen and admired all over the world. Married to actress Sinead Cusack, Irons keeps his private family life closely guarded from the prying eyes of the press, only revealing himself in his various performing guises.

ROBERT MAXWELL

Mr Maxwell came to this country as an immigrant from Czechoslovakia at the age of seventeen.
He enlisted in the armed forces for the Second World War, which he completed as a captain,
having been awarded the Military Cross. After the war he founded Pergamon Press, which has
become one of the largest publishing empires in the world. He is currently Chairman of the
Mirror Group (*Mirror, Sunday Mirror, People, etc.*) as well as Chairman of Derby County
and Oxford United FCs.

ALAN SUGAR

Who would have dreamed fifteen years ago of the day when every home would think of a micro-computer as a possession as ordinary as a washing machine or a television set? Alan Sugar is a man who has done much to bring this dream to reality. In 1968, at the age of twenty-one, he founded Amstrad, a company of which he is still chairman. Amstrad's computers, selling for as little as £400, have in the 1980s created a revolution in our ability to record, store and retrieve words, facts and figures.

PETER FLUCK and ROGER LAW

Creators of the puppets for the wickedly satirical and enormously popular television series *Spitting Image*, Peter Fluck and Roger Law have been in partnership since 1975. They have for some years worked mainly as makers of models used to illustrate magazine personality profiles. Their television series began in 1984 and has won audiences of over fourteen million in this country, as well as a world-wide following which proves the exportability of British humour!

SIR KENNETH NEWMAN

Commissioner of the Metropolitan Police 1982-7, Sir Kenneth Newman is a fervently reforming crime-fighter, with extensive experience of the world's trouble-spots, having worked in both the Palestine Police (1946-8) and the Royal Ulster Constabulary (1973-9). It is to him, for instance, that we owe much of the growth of 'Neighbourhood Watch' schemes.

PENELOPE KEITH

Penelope Keith is one of those actresses whom the theatre-going public have known and loved for many years. She came to the public's attention first in her snobby middle-class role as Sarah in *The Norman Conquests*. So successful was her performance that an entire television series was recreated around it. *The Good Life* extended her reputation from thousands of theatregoers to millions of TV viewers. The millions laughed at her superbly portrayed role because they knew she represented the multitude of middle-class achievers who make up the Britain of the eighties.

SAMANTHA FOX

One of the *Sun's* prettiest page 3 girls, Samantha was their Girl of the Year three years in succession. Quite a record. She has recently brought out her first record, *Touch Me*, which has been number one in the charts in seventeen countries.

PROFESSOR MAGDI HABIB YACOUB

Professor Magdi Yacoub, an expert in heart and heart-lung transplants, is in charge of the busiest transplant unit in Europe at Harefield Hospital. When he has time to spare from his very exacting operating schedule he enjoys gardening, growing orchids and listening to classical music.

SIR ROY CALNE

Transplant surgery is one of the most complex, sophisticated and exciting areas of modern medicine. Sir Roy Calne is one of the leading figures in the field: he trained at Guy's Hospital, London and, since 1965, has been Professor of Surgery at Cambridge University, where he is also a Fellow of Trinity Hall College. He was awarded the Lister Medal in 1984.

SIR NICHOLAS GOODISON

Few men can manage to maintain real distinction in two radically different fields of endeavour, but one such is Sir Nicholas Goodison. Chairman of the Stock Exchange since 1976, presiding over a period of great change in the City, he is also a scholar in the history of English furniture and decorative arts, who has published definitive books on English barometers and ormolu.

JAMES STIRLING

Trained at the Liverpool School of Art and a paratrooper at the D-Day landing in Normandy, James Stirling is one of the world's leading architects. Among his most innovative buildings are the History Library at Cambridge University and the art gallery at Stuttgart. The Clore Gallery, designed by James Stirling to house the J.M.W. Turner collection, was opened in 1987.

SIR JOHN GIELGUD

One of the greatest actors of the century. He will probably be remembered more for his voice than for any individual performance. However, those who were lucky enough to see the great years at the Old Vic, when he and Laurence Olivier played Iago and Othello on alternate nights, may not agree with this statement. Sir John has given so many virtuoso performances during the last decade that it is virtually impossible to single any one out, although this writer would queue to see him repeat *The Seven Ages of Man*.

DAME PEGGY ASHCROFT

Miss Ashcroft is undoubtedly our leading lady of the British theatre. In a career that has spanned sixty years, she has played almost every female lead in the British theatre. During the eighties she gave a memorable performance as Barbie in *The Jewel in the Crown*, which was followed by the Oscar-winning Mrs Moore in *A Passage to India*. She is among those few giants of her profession that have a theatre named after her. It seems impossible to believe that she has been a Dame for over thirty years.

LORD HAILSHAM

Barrister and politician by profession, Lord Hailsham was the longest serving Cabinet minister since the Second World War. Chairman of the Conservative Party, Lord President of the Council and Lord Chancellor are three of the high offices he held during his fifty years in both Houses of Parliament. As a young man he was considered to be the finest orator of his generation. He sought once to gain the leadership of the Conservative Party and premiership in 1963, but the 'magic circle' (before every Member of Parliament had a vote) selected Sir Alec Douglas-Home.

SIR GEOFFREY HOWE

Geoffrey Howe is a Welshman born in Port Talbot who won an exhibition to Winchester and a scholarship to Trinity Hall, Cambridge. He is one of those rare politicians who have few, if any, enemies. He served in several ministerial posts in the last three Tory administrations, and more recently as Chancellor of the Exchequer in the first Thatcher government and Foreign Secretary in the second one. A man never underestimated by those who have worked closely with him, Sir Geoffrey is taking on the role that Lord Butler held in the Tory party in the fifties and sixties.

DENIS THATCHER

Denis Thatcher has been a director of several companies including Burma Oil, and has proved to be a successful business man over the past thirty years. In his younger days he was a first class rugby union football referee, and he has remained a fervent supporter of the game on and off the field. A firm believer in the old amateur ideals, he scorns the modern moves in professional sport. After his retirement he took up residence in No 10 Downing Street.

JIMMY YOUNG

Jimmy Young, a former pop singer, is now the king of the disc jockeys. He interviews Cabinet Ministers and celebrities in a unique combination of phone-in and direct questions. He is a great favourite of Margaret Thatcher who has been on his TV programme several times.

DAVID FROST

A failed opening batsman and inside half, Mr Frost has settled for being a television producer and presenter. Immediately after leaving Cambridge he became the star of *That Was The Week That Was*, and since then he has refused to go away. A generous man with a phenomenal memory and unquestioned ability, heaven knows what he will get up to in the nineties.

SELINA SCOTT

Selina Scott's combination of brains and beauty has made her one of the most popular television personalities of the 1980s. She joined television in 1977, after reading English and American studies at the University of East Anglia. After some years in journalism she moved to ITN and won fame as a newscaster; then, in 1982, she helped to launch the BBC's 'Breakfast Time' television.

BRUCE OLDFIELD

Brought up in a Doctor Barnardo's home, Bruce Oldfield went on to study at St Martin's College of Art before swiftly establishing himself as one of the world's most stylish and inventive fashion designers. He numbers among his clients many celebrities, not least the Princess of Wales. Bruce's good humour, generosity and work for charity have won him further friends and admirers all over the world.

MORRISSEY

Since their hit record 'This Charming Man' in 1982, The Smiths have proved themselves to be one of the most tough and exciting bands in British rock music. Their lead singer and lyrics writer Manchester-born Morrissey (he never uses his Christian name of Steven) is a genuine street poet, fascinated by Oscar Wilde and his novel *The Picture of Dorian Gray*. He has become a grim commentator on the perils of modern urban life.

DEREK JACOBI

Derek Jacobi has appeared in a long list of successful plays and films since his debut on the stage of the Birmingham Repertory Theatre in 1961. He is known for his masterly portrayal of Claudius in the television series *I Claudius* and for the title role of *Cyrano de Bergerac*.

SINEAD CUSACK

Sinead Cusack comes from a well-known theatrical family. She is the daughter of Cyril Cusack and is married to Jeremy Irons. Television, films and the live theatre are all grist to her mill. Her first appearance in London was opposite Donald Sinden in the Royal Shakespeare Company's *London Assurance* and in 1984 she appeared on Broadway in *Cyrano* and *Much Ado About Nothing*, for which she won a Tony Award.

SIR IAN MACGREGOR

Sir Ian, who is now with Lazards, will be best remembered for his leadership of the steel, and subsequently the coal, industries. When he was Chairman of the National Coal Board he took on and beat the Miners Strike in 1985. He is a poor communicator, but a good administrator. He was inaccurately described by the Bishop of Durham as a 'foreign septuagenarian'. He is a proud Scot.

JENNIFER D'ABO

Jennifer d'Abo is quite simply a woman tycoon. She was Chairman of Ryman until it was taken over by Pentos. She had turned it into a profitable and efficient business. She is also a director of the London Docklands Development Corporation and Channel Four Television. Quite a girl.

GEMMA LEVINE

Gemma Levine, the talented photographer who took the portraits in this book, made an impact in 1978 when Weidenfeld & Nicolson published two books of her work *Israel's Faces and Places* and *Living with the Bible*. She then went on to produce three books on Henry Moore. Before starting work on *Faces of the 80s* she had a major exhibition on Israel. She is a perfectionist in everything she does. This portrait of her was taken by Peter Bowles.

PETER BOWLES

For those of us who have watched *Rumpole of the Bailey*, *To the Manor Born*, and *The Irish RM*, Peter Bowles is the epitomy of the slightly snobby gentleman who (so the rest of the world imagines) personifies the Englishman at his best—and worst. For thirty years he has given superb performances on the stage, starting with a debut at the Old Vic in 1956.

ARCHBISHOP OF CANTERBURY

Robert Runcie is the only Archbishop to have won the Military Cross. His appointment as
Archbishop of Canterbury was something of a surprise, as previously he had only been Bishop of
St Albans. His voice when preaching is somewhat flat and deadpan. However, to talk to, in
private, he is witty, humorous, totally without pomposity and has a great deal of charm.

ANNABELLE

SIR PETER HALL

Sir Peter Hall has been the Director of the National Theatre since 1963, having been formerly a director of the Royal Shakespeare Company. He took over his post at the National Theatre from Laurence Olivier, and guided it through financial turmoil and political setbacks until today it is the most respected theatre company in the world. So many award-winning productions bear his name, that one would need a glossary to list them.

LORD WEIDENFELD

Lord Weidenfeld is best known as Harold Wilson's publisher. Wilson used him on a personal mission to Hubert Humphrey, then the American Vice-President, to see if the CIA was working against him when he was Prime Minister. He is an ardent Jew and in 1948 he spent a year as Political Advisor and Chief of Cabinet to President Weizman of Israel. Weidenfeld & Nicholson, of which he is the Chairman, is one of the top publishing houses in Europe.

TIMOTHY DALTON

Darkly handsome Timothy Dalton has long been well known to British theatre- and cinema-goers for his fine performances in a wide range of classic and modern plays, including a memorable portrayal of Richard the Lionheart in *The Lion in Winter*, where he more than held his own opposite his co-stars Peter O'Toole and Katharine Hepburn. But in 1987 he reached an altogether new level of fame, when he took over the role of the most glamorous undercover agent of them all—Ian Fleming's James Bond, alias 007—in the film *The Living Daylights*.

STEWART STEVEN

One of the great success stories of British journalism in the 1980s is the *Mail on Sunday*. Its editor since 1982 has been Stewart Steven, who came to the job after an impressive apprenticeship with the *Daily Express*, where he was foreign editor, and the *Daily Mail*, where he was associate editor from 1974 to 1982. Stewart Steven is also the author of three books, including one on the people of Poland.

ALAN BATES

Alan Bates is in every sense of the word a man of the eighties, a contemporary actor who has made his name in modern films and theatre. Over the past decade he has won several major awards for performances such as the father in *A Day in the Death of Joe Egg* and Guy Burgess in *An Englishman Abroad.*

ELAINE PAGE

Starting her career in the chorus for *Hair* and *Jesus Christ Superstar,* Elaine Page had her decisive break as Eva Peron in the Andrew Lloyd Webber-Tim Rice musical *Evita* in 1978. She has continued her associations with them through performances as Grisabella in Lloyd Webber's *Cats* and Florence in Tim Rice's *Chess.* 'Don't cry for me, Argentina', 'Memory' and 'I know him so well' are indelibly linked to her vibrant and sensuous voice.

RICHARD ROGERS

A modernist visionary, Richard Rogers has designed two of the most dazzling showpiece buildings of the century. Rogers' designs for the Centre Pompidou, 'the Beaubourg', in Paris were chosen from competition with nearly seven hundred other architects; since its opening in 1977 the building has been visited by over a million people a year. In London, the Lloyds' building (opened by the Queen in 1986) has proved very controversial—but no one can deny its breathtaking impact. He is now working on a conversion of Billingsgate Market for Citibank.

SIR HUGH CASSON

During the greater part of the eighties Sir Hugh Casson was President of the Royal Academy. A distinguished water colourist, during his period as President he brought the Academy back into public prominence. It was sad to discover, on the opening day of the Summer Exhibition, that Sir Hugh's pictures had been sold even before we had climbed to the main gallery. One of the things for which he will be most remembered is that he kept his pictures in the price range that made it possible for most modest collectors to hang them on their walls.

BRYAN ROBSON

One of the most dazzling footballers of the 1980s, Bryan Robson has been captain of both England and Manchester United. Like his name-sake (but no relation) Bobby Robson, Bryan hails from County Durham and at one time played for West Bromwich Albion— from which his transfer fee to Manchester was a staggering £1½ million.

BOBBY ROBSON

A man in the hot seat is Bobby Robson, manager and coach for England's football team—a job where you have to be ready to bear most of the blame while receiving little of the credit. Bobby Robson knows the business from the inside, however, having played professionally for Fulham and West Bromwich Albion, and made twenty appearances for England. Before being appointed to the England post he was manager of Ipswich Town. One of his recreations is the uncompetitive one of sheep farming.

CAREY LABOVITCH

In 1986, at the age of twenty-one, Carey Labovitch was the youngest ever finalist in the Business Woman of the Year Award, and undoubtedly the youngest mainstream magazine publisher in the country. Her best-known publication to date is *Blitz*, a glamorous, hard-hitting and nippily written magazine of music, fashion and style—an ongoing documentary of young British culture and its considerable energies. Carey started the magazine while still an undergraduate at Oxford, and within a year had led it to its first award (for best graphics) and a nationwide circulation.

DR DANNIE ABSE

Dr Abse has been President of the Poetry Society since 1979 and has for the past decade been a prolific writer of poetry, plays and novels. His latest collection of poetry was *Ask the Bloody Horse*, 1986. For those of you who think that is all he is doing, Dr Abse is a specialist in charge of the chest clinic at the Central Medical Establishment, a post which he has held since 1954.
His brother Leo is a distinguished lawyer and a former Member of Parliament.

SIR JEREMY MORSE

Sir Jeremy Morse has been Chairman of Lloyds Bank since 1977 and is one of our most able bankers. He is known worldwide through having been Alternate Governor for the United Kingdom on the International Monetary Fund. His listed recreations include problems and puzzles, particularly appropriate for a banker.

SIR JOHN HARVEY-JONES

Sir John Harvey-Jones, innovative and inspirational leader of ICI from 1982 to 1987, is credited with turning round this largest of Britain's industrial companies, increasing its value fivefold. This followed a distinguished twenty-year career in the Royal Navy. A jovial, generous spirited individualist, he is Chancellor of Bradford University and vigorously espouses many causes.

DAME JANET BAKER

Dame Janet Baker is one of the world's most sought after opera singers, is the President of the Royal Scottish Academy of Music and Drama and a member of the Munster Trust. Her long and successful career has earned her a prominent place among the most distinguished artists Britain has ever produced. There are few nations on earth she has not performed in and been honoured by. She enjoys reading and tennis.

SIMON RATTLE

A musical wonder boy, Simon Rattle is one of the most brilliant orchestral conductors that this country has produced. Principal Conductor of the City of Birmingham Symphony Orchestra and a regular guest with Glyndebourne and the Los Angeles Philharmonic Orchestra, Rattle was awarded the CBE. His recorded performances of Mahler, Sibelius, Britten, and French music rank with those of the greatest masters, yet he is also innovatory in his music.

NORMAN PARKINSON

If Buckingham Palace were ever to institute the office of 'Photographer Royal', a front runner would be Norman Parkinson. He has taken portraits of all members of the Royal Family—including the engagement photographs for Prince Charles and Lady Diana Spencer, and the eightieth and eighty-fifth birthday photographs of the Queen Mother. Also a notable fashion photographer, he creates images of romance and glamour—even though his leisure-time activities are the rather more down-to-earth ones of pig farming and breeding Creole racehorses.

DR JONATHAN MILLER

Jonathan Miller combines a career as a doctor with that of author and director of stage and television. He got his taste for the footlights when he was co-author and participator in *Beyond the Fringe*. An exceptionally talented man, he lists his recreation as 'deep sleep', which must make him the envy of every insomniac.

ANDREAS WHITTAM SMITH

Andreas Whittam Smith is the Editor and founder of *The Independent*, the first serious daily to have started its life in the 1980s. Having been on the *Daily Telegraph*, the *Financial Times* and *The Times*, he has had a good schooling in journalism. A man of courage, he committed criminal contempt by publishing a full front-page extract from Spycatcher. He was the first editor to risk going to jail because of his passionate belief in the freedom of the Press. *The Independent* won the Newspaper of the Year award.

CHARLES WILSON

Charles Wilson started his journalistic career on the old *News Chronicle*. He is the third editor of *The Times* under Rupert Murdoch's ownership, succeeding Charles Douglas-Home who tragically died at an early age. He is a Glaswegian by birth and enjoys reading and horse racing.

DR RICHARD SMITH

Many changes in medical thought have occurred in the 1980s, and one of the doctors who has done most to bring them to the public is Dr Richard Smith, who for four years was BBC's *Breakfast Time* consultant doctor. He is also an assistant editor of the *British Medical Journal*, and a prolific writer and broadcaster. His forceful and direct treatment of what he considers to be the health scourges of our time—be they alcohol or unemployment—has involved him in considerable controversy.

JOHN HAYES

If the National Portrait Gallery has the enviable reputation of being one of the brightest and most engrossing of our national museums, then a good deal of the credit must go to John Hayes, its Director since 1974. Previously Director of the London Museum and a Visiting Professor in History of Art at Yale University, John Hayes has written many books on English art and artists, including notable monographs on Gainsborough, Rowlandson and Graham Sutherland.

DAME ELIZABETH FRINK

Like all great sculptors, Dame Elizabeth's work can be spotted at 100 yards. It has a distinctive quality and style that cannot be mistaken for anyone else's—the quality of originality. Perhaps best known for her magnificent sculptures of horses, her work can be seen in almost every major gallery in the world.

SIR JOHN MILLS

One of Britain's most talented actor/producer/directors, Sir John first appeared on stage in 1929. One of his earliest performances was in Noel Coward's *Cavalcade* but he will be best remembered for countless roles in British war films. His breakthrough came after a remarkable performance in *Hobson's Choice*. Perhaps his greatest triumph and one which won him an Oscar was his performance in David Lean's *Ryan's Daughter*—a part in which he never spoke.

BOB HOSKINS

Never destined to play Romeo or James Bond, Bob Hoskins has proved that real ability can overcome many minor disadvantages. He won several awards for his brilliant performance as Nathan Detroit in *Guys and Dolls*, and more recently was nominated for an Oscar for his role as Marker in *Mona Lisa*. He did not win, but no doubt the problem will be solved in the nineties.

MELVYN BRAGG

Melvyn Bragg is a Cumberland man who, during the eighties, has been one of the most successful presenters of the more serious films and plays to be brought to the British television screen. He is also a distinguished novelist, whose most recent book reached the number one spot on the *Sunday Times* best seller list—a fatal achievement for someone who wishes to be taken seriously. As a loyal fan of Carlisle United, he is obviously a man who supports lost causes.

TERRY WOGAN

Terry Wogan became a household name when he did a marathon twelve months on an early morning Radio 2 programme. He was seven times the *TV Times* TV Personality of the Year and he now has his own chat show three times a week on BBC 1. He interviews his guests in a comfortable and relaxed manner, rarely probing too deeply, but was rather disconcerted by Princess Anne when she appeared on his programme and began to interview him.

NIGEL HAWTHORNE

Nigel Hawthorne returned to England from South Africa in 1951 and, with the exception of a few engagements abroad, has worked here ever since, both on stage and in television. It is, however, as Sir Humphrey in *Yes, Minister* and *Yes, Prime Minister* that he has made an eradicable place for himself in the eighties. He was awarded the CBE in 1986.

LORD SOPER

Lord Soper is eighty-four years young. A Methodist minister and a Labour Life Peer, he is best known for addressing large gatherings at Speaker's Corner and Tower Hill. He puts down all hecklers fairly, but with good humour. He once said to a heckler at Speaker's Corner 'As a Christian, I love you, but I don't like you'.

JANET SUZMAN

South African-born actress Janet Suzman has played many of the great classical roles for the Royal Shakespeare Company—including Rosalind, Hedda Gabler and Cleopatra—to which she has brought a fiery intelligence and warmth embodying a very modern sort of womanhood. In 1986 she had great success in Dennis Potter's television series *The Singing Detective*. Cinemagoers will also remember her touching portrayal of the last Czarina in *Nicholas and Alexandra*.

DAVID MONEY-COUTTS

David Money-Coutts has been Chairman of Coutts & Company since 1976 and has spent his life in banking and finance. Despite the fact that Coutts are now part of the National Westminster Group, he presides over their head office, which resembles a tropical garden. Like all his staff, he still wears a frock coat when he greets customers. Appropriately, as a banker, his wife's name is Penny.

MARMADUKE HUSSEY

'Duke' Hussey was appointed Chairman of the Board of Governors of the BBC in 1986, although he has spent most of his working life in newspapers. His wife, Lady Susan Hussey, has been a Lady-in-Waiting to the Queen since 1960. A husband with a foot in Fleet Street and a wife with a foot in Buckingham Palace is a highly unusual combination.

FRANK MUIR

A genuinely witty man whose sharp humour is based on a great deal of knowledge and experience. Millions have enjoyed his rivalry with Denis Norden in *Face the Music* and in *Call my Bluff*. For those of you who have only seen him sitting down, he is 6 ft 4 in.

JASPER CARROTT

Jasper Carrott is one of our great comic originals, in a line that stretches from Chaplin to Cleese. His fast street-wise humour, full of sharp human observation and whiplash wit, has made him one of the BBC's hottest television properties. And its not just in Britain that he is appreciated—from Hong Kong to Los Angeles, Madrid to Dubai, everyone seems to see the joke in whacky Jasper Carrott.

VISCOUNT ALTHORP

Lord Althorp retired as a Page of Honour to the Queen in 1979. The eighties have seen him taking up a serious career in American television. As the brother of the Princess of Wales he is pestered by the popular press but, although only twenty-three, he knows exactly how to handle journalists. He likes flying, rugby, cricket and acting. He has, finally, arrived socially by becoming the step-grandson of Barbara Cartland.

RICHARD SEIFERT

Mr Richard Seifert, one of Britain's most distinguished architects, can travel from the City of London to the West End and see a building he has designed every sixty seconds. There is also not one capital in the EEC that does not boast a Seifert building. Among the buildings that are national landmarks are the Wembley Conference Centre, the Royal Garden Hotel and numerous hospitals. He has taken a great interest in many medical charities and in London University.

LORD CAMPBELL OF ESKAN

Jock Campbell is one of those tough Scots who, had he been at his peak in the 1880s, would undoubtedly have been our Governor General in one of Her Majesty's far-flung colonies. As a modern Brit he has been President of the Town Planning Association since 1980, and some would say the founding father of Milton Keynes—indeed, he became its first Freeman. As Chairman of Booker McConnell, the publishing company which handles such authors as Ian Fleming and Agatha Christie, he also played a great part in the founding of the Booker Prize.

SIR LAWRIE BARRATT

A 'Barratt' home has become synonymous with solid craftsmanship and simple elegant architectural design. Behind that reputation is Sir Lawrie Barratt, Chairman and Managing Director of Barratt Developments, a company he founded in 1958 — and the success of which brought him a knighthood in 1982.

HELENA BONHAM-CARTER

Helena Bonham-Carter is the great granddaughter of the Liberal Prime Minister, Herbert Asquith, whose term of office has only been exceeded by that of Margaret Thatcher. It is in the eighties that Helena has made her mark as a television and film actress. She will, of course, be best remembered as the heroine in E. M. Forster's *A Room With a View*.

JASPER CONRAN

Jasper Conran has become one of the leading names in fashion in the eighties. His first collection, however, was in New York for Henri Bendel. The range of his work extends through shoes, lingerie and menswear. One of his specialities has been to design cashmeres for the Scotch House. He is the son of Sir Terence Conran and Shirley Conran.

NEIL KINNOCK

Neil Kinnock, like Geoffrey Howe, is a Welshman, but there the similarity ends. Mr Kinnock has the brilliant oratorical skills that one associates with Nye Bevan and Michael Foot. He has striven hard to hold together the modern Labour Party, which proved to be a hard task for Jim Callaghan and Lord Wilson before him. Despite this, he took a more united Labour Party into the 1987 election than anyone would have thought possible a year earlier, and indeed political pundits of every colour considered that he ran a masterful campaign.

DR DAVID OWEN

Dr David Owen has represented a Plymouth constituency since 1966, first as a socialist, then as a member of the SDP, and heaven knows what in the nineties. He was James Callaghan's surprise choice as Foreign Secretary, following the premature death of Anthony Crosland in 1977, but after the Labour Party lost the election in 1979, along with Roy Jenkins, Shirley Williams and Bill Rodgers, he founded the SDP in 1981. After the 1983 election he took over the leadership from Roy Jenkins, a position he held until his resignation in 1987. He will surely play a major role in the nineties.

DAVID STEEL

David Steel became a Scottish Member of Parliament in 1965, and succeeded Jeremy Thorpe as leader of the Liberal Party in 1976. In 1978 he formed the Lib/Lab pact with James Callaghan, which enabled the Labour Party to remain in power. In 1983 he formed an Alliance with the SDP in order that they could fight the general election in every seat without being rivals. In 1987 he was the motivator behind the merger of the SDP and Liberal parties into one party. It remains to be seen whether he will lead that combined grouping into the next general election.

SEBASTIAN COE

This 5ft 9in, 9-stone man is one of the giants of modern athletics. He has thirteen world records during the decade, and he is the only athlete in the history of the modern Olympics to have retained the 1500-metre title, having won it in Moscow in 1980. More recently he has been appointed Vice-Chairman of the Sports Council. I suspect that, if this book is reissued in the nineties, we shall read that Sebastian Coe is a politician who as a young man was an athlete.

STEVE DAVIS

Steve Davis has dominated the snooker world in the eighties. Three times he has been world champion, and he has headed the ranking lists since 1981. Still only thirty years old, one cannot imagine that he will not dominate the nineties and happily continue to do so into the next century, as the world's greatest player.

NICK FALDO

Nick Faldo shot to prominence with his victory in the British Open Golf Championship this year but, like all sportsmen who take a major honour, there have been years of hard work and minor victories the general public have been unaware of. During the eighties he has won ten professional titles, including the Spanish Open Championship.

FELICITY LOTT

Felicity Lott, the well-known soprano, has sung in principal roles with the English National Opera, Glyndebourne, the Welsh National Opera, and Covent Garden. She has also appeared in operatic roles in Europe and in recitals, concerts and oratorios. She is a founder member of the *Song Makers Almanac*, and enjoys cooking, reading and dressmaking.

MICHAEL PARKINSON

A Yorkshireman first and foremost who has failed completely in his ambition to open the batting for England and play as centre forward for Barnsley. His second choice of profession has, however, proved to be immensely successful. He started life as a journalist in the north of England before coming up to the capital to work for London Weekend Television as a sports presenter. Soon after followed his successful television interviews of personalities, mainly from films, theatre and sport. He has most recently taken over the role of presenter of *Desert Island Discs*.

ALAN SILLITOE

Alan Sillitoe's hard-hitting and revealing novels of working-class people, such as *The Loneliness of the Long-Distance Runner* and *Saturday Night and Sunday Morning*, were enormously influential on the course of fiction when they were first published in the late 1950s and 1960s. Still a prolific writer in many literary genres, Sillitoe has recently had enormous success at another end of the market with his lighthearted 'Marmalade Jim' books for children.

SIR JOHN TOOLEY

Opera and ballet are expensive and difficult to mount to international standards, and Sir John Tooley's achievement in maintaining the status of the Royal Opera House, Covent Garden, cannot be underestimated. Appointed General Administrator in 1970, Sir John has proved a superb diplomat. His visionary management has also opened up the opera house to new audiences.

HENRY WRONG

Henry Wrong, a Canadian by birth, has had a fantastic career, starting at Glyndebourne and taking on, among other things, the stage and business administration of the Metropolitan Opera Association in New York. A brilliant administrator, he is now the popular Director of the Barbican Centre. He is fascinated by old houses and antiques, and is a keen gardener. He has recently become a Fishmonger.

PROFESSOR ALAN BOWNESS

Alan Bowness, Director of the Tate Gallery since 1980, has published numerous works on modern painting and sculpture. He is famous both in North and South America as well as Britain. He enjoys listening to music, reading, especially poetry and nineteenth century fiction.

PAUL FOX

Paul Fox is probably the most respected man in British television today, but because he is always behind the·scenes, he is virtually unknown to the British public. He spent his early career as a journalist before becoming editor of *Sportsview* and then on to *Panorama*. Just when he was tipped to be Director General of the BBC, he left to become Managing Director of Yorkshire Television.

JEREMY ISAACS

Channel Four is one of the great success stories of the British media in the 1980s, and much of the credit for its high quality of programming must go to its first Chief Executive Jeremy Isaacs, who in 1985 was justly deemed worthy of the Lord Willis Award for Distinguished Service to Television. In 1987 it was announced that Isaacs would make a dramatic change of direction and succeed Sir John Tooley as the General Administrator of the Royal Opera House, Covent Garden.

FIONA SHAW

Elegant, willowy and acidly witty, actress Fiona Shaw has garnered a dazzling set of rave reviews since winning the Tree Award at RADA in 1982. From a memorable portrayal of Mary Shelley in Howard Brenton's play *Bloody Poetry* to many original performances for the Royal Shakespeare Company, Fiona has proved herself one of those actresses who always defies expectations. Undoubtedly among our most talented actresses in Britain today.

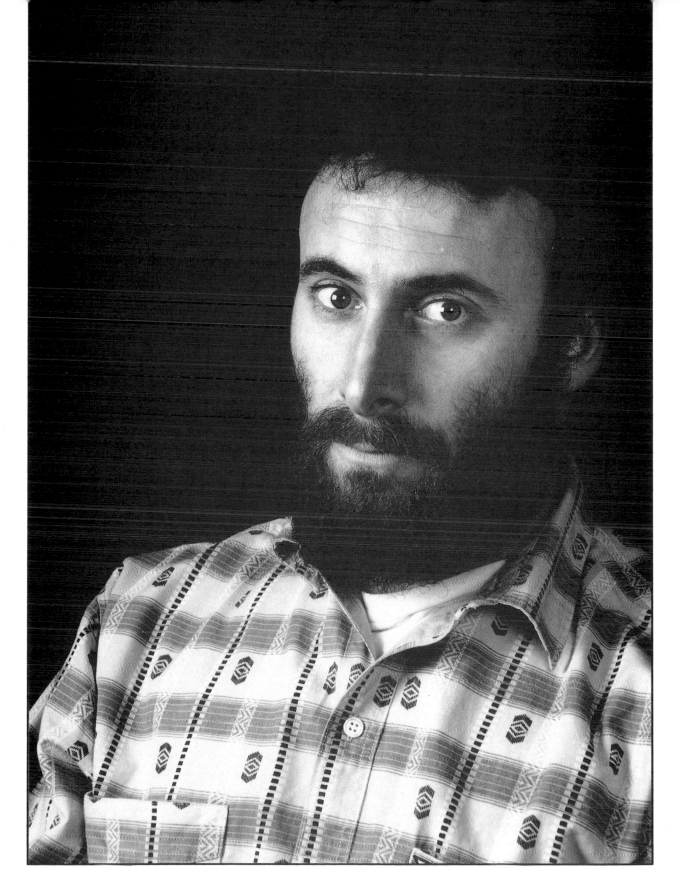

ANTONY SHER

An uncannily brilliant impersonator of everyone from Arab businessmen to American drag queens, South African-born, RADA-trained actor Antony Sher has had every superlative lavished upon him, including the inevitable comparison with Laurence Olivier. Sher combines intensity, a streak of demoniac humour, with an astonishing physical energy plus a fine ear for the subtleties of Shakespearean verse. In his book *Year of the King*, he has memorably described his experiences of rehearsing and performing Richard III.

— JOHN MORTIMER —

A brilliant barrister notable for his defence of many liberal causes—particularly those associated with censorship and civil liberties—John Mortimer has also had a glittering career as a writer. He has adapted the work of others for both stage and television as well as originating his own scripts. His novel *Paradise Postponed* was also turned into a successful television series in 1986.

— SIR CLIVE SINCLAIR —

Sir Clive Sinclair is an eccentric. Leaving school at sixteen, he has employed more first class scientific minds than most universities. His refinement of the modern computer and calculator has made him a leader in the electronics field. He has been heralded and written off so often during the eighties that there can be no doubt he will have a major role to play in the nineties. His love of jogging (very slowly) and of music are well known to anyone who lives in the Cambridge area.

ANTHONY DOWELL

Anthony Dowell has been Director of the Royal Ballet, Covent Garden, since 1986 and has been its senior principal dancer since 1966. He has danced in all the major productions and has toured all over the world with them, particularly in Russia and the United States. The world of ballet is his whole life.

BRYONY BRIND

Bryony Brind was only a student in 1978 when she accompanied the Royal Ballet on its tour of Korea and America. She won the 1981 Olivier (Benson & Hedges) Award for the outstanding first achievement of the year in ballet. She partnered Rudolf Nureyev in *La Bayadere* and has been described by some critics as one of the most exciting dancers of her generation.

LORD YOUNG OF GRAFFAM

Lord Young is Secretary of State for Trade and Industry and before that he was Secretary of State for Employment. He is every inch a Margaret Thatcher man. Plucked from the Manpower Services the Prime Minister gave him a peerage and a seat in the Cabinet. She says of him 'Everybody else brings me problems. David brings me answers'. His love of opera has caused him to miss the occasional vote in the House of Commons.

LORD FORTE

'Charlie', as the public know him, is a 5 ft 4 in giant who always claims he won the Olympic long jump while trying to throw the hammer. Nothing sums up his character better, for during the last thirty years he has built up one of Britain's most successful catering companies. His support of good causes is legendary, and he became Baron Forte of Ripley in 1982.

BRENDA DEAN

The first woman to become Secretary General of a major trade union (SOGAT). During the eighties it has been her responsibility to lead a union that has had to face the biggest changes in modern management. Her calm, unruffled appearances on television made her a popular figure in an unpopular cause, and although she did not win every battle she made few enemies.

NORMAN WILLIS

Norman Willis, the cheerful, cuddly General Secretary of the TUC, succeeded the cadavorous Len Murray. He was clearly chosen to show the British the nice face of trade unionism.

SIR RALPH HALPERN

Sir Ralph developed the first example of market segmentation strategy with the Top Shop for
Peter Robinson in the 1960s. He became Chairman and Chief Executive of the Burton Group in
1981 and has turned the group into one of the largest in the UK, accounting for almost ten per
cent of the clothing market. He is the highest paid executive in Great Britain, earning over
£1 000 000 a year.

CECIL PARKINSON

Cecil Parkinson was the architect of the Conservative landslide victory in 1983 and was appointed Secretary of State for Trade and Industry in the same year. He resigned after the revelation that his secretary was to give birth to their child. He continued to be an active supporter of the Prime Minister and was appointed Secretary of State for Energy in 1987. He was a Cambridge athletics Blue, and during his years in the wilderness continued to take an interest in athletics by becoming a director of the Sports Aid Foundation.

SIMON CALLOW

Simon Callow shot to fame when he played the part of Mozart in Peter Shaffer's play *Amadeus*, first seen at London's National Theatre in 1979. Since then he has established himself as one of the most intelligent and versatile character actors of his generation, with a special gift for the wittier brands of comedy and a rare ability to be equally effective on stage, film, and television. Very much an individualist, Simon Callow's views on the acting profession were controversially aired in his book *Being an Actor*.

BRUCE KENT

When Monsignor Bruce Kent became private secretary to the Archbishop of Westminster in 1963, at the age of thirty-four, he seemed to be destined for a Bishopric, and possibly even the see of Westminster, which traditionally carries with it a Cardinal's hat. But it was not to be. In 1980, after several important ecclesiastical posts, he became General Secretary for the Campaign for Nuclear Disarmament. Despite the tolerance of Cardinal Hume, he left the priesthood in 1987. Now Vice-Chairman of CND he seems likely to spend the rest of the 1980s campaigning for peace.

DR MIRIAM STOPPARD

A qualified doctor and specialist in dermatology, Miriam Stoppard is married to playwright Tom Stoppard. She is a popular television personality, presenting *Where There's Life* and *Woman to Woman*, as well as the author of lucid and commonsensical books on health and baby care.

TOM STOPPARD

Arguably our most distinguished living playwright, with such plays as *Rosencrantz and Guildenstern are Dead, Jumpers* and *The dog it was that Died*. He has won almost every major literary award in Britain and America, and has recently turned his hand to film television scripts and adaptations of foreign playwrights. Perhaps the most staggering thing about Mr Stoppard is that English is not his native tongue.

TIMOTHY WEST and PRUNELLA SCALES

It would be impossible to list adequately all the achievements of this highly talented theatrical couple. On television, Timothy West is probably best known for playing Winston Churchill in *Churchill and the Generals*. Everyone will remember Prunella Scales as Sybil in *Fawlty Towers* and Mapp in *Mapp and Lucia*. They gave delightfully amusing performances when they played together recently in Priestley's *When We are Married*.

HOWARD HODGKIN

Howard Hodgkin is one of our major painters and has exhibited in all the leading galleries in Britain. He has also exhibited in the United States, Australia, Canada, India, Japan and in most countries in Western Europe. In 1985 he won the Turner Prize.

NICOLA HICKS

Nicola Hicks was picked by Dame Elizabeth Frink as the most promising newcomer in the 1984 Artist of the Day exhibition. She works in clay, straw and plaster, and charcoal on brown paper. Her subjects are mostly animals.

THE DUKE OF WESTMINSTER

Gerald Grosvenor inherited his title from his father who, as Colonel Robert Grosvenor, sat in the House of Commons. He is one of the richest men in the world and is said to have an income of £15,000 an hour. He runs the Grosvenor Estates, is involved with many charities and was Chairman of the Centenary Appeal of the NSPCC. He is a modest and charming young man.

ROBIN LEIGH-PEMBERTON

Governor of the Bank of England since 1983 and Lord Lieutenant of Kent since 1982, Robin Leigh-Pemberton is a notable figure in English public life, who serves on many national committees. A former Grenadier Guard, he is a trustee of Glyndebourne Arts Trust and a seneschal of Canterbury Cathedral.

THOMAS ALLEN

One of the most popular and gifted figures in the musical world today, baritone Thomas Allen, who hails from County Durham, delights audiences worldwide with his forthright and virile interpretations of the title-roles in such operas as *The Barber of Seville*, *Eugene Onegin*, *Billy Budd*, and *The Marriage of Figaro*. An electrifying actor as well as a virtuoso singer, Thomas Allen has made many recordings, and is as acclaimed on the stages of the prestigious Metropolitan Opera in New York and the Opéra in Paris as he is 'at home' in Covent Garden.

PHILIP LANGRIDGE and ANN MURRAY

Tenor Philip Langridge and mezzo-soprano Ann Murray manage to be both married and at the top of their profession—though they have rarely sung on stage together. Famous for his interpretations of twentieth-century music, Langridge recently took part in the first performance of Harrison Birtwistle's vast and difficult *The Mask of Orpheus*, for the English National Opera. Miss Murray has had standing ovations in many of the great musical centres of the world and is particularly noted as a singer of the music of Mozart and Richard Strauss.

GODFREY BRADMAN

Mr Bradman is one of those rare examples of a highly successful man who is generally unknown. Over the past decade he has built one of the most respected and successful property companies in the UK, but his first interest has always been philanthropic pursuits. His work for such bodies as Shelter and the Society for the Protection of the Unborn Child has proved invaluable to both societies. His latest venture is in a research programme for AIDS where his generosity, coupled with determination, will surely once again prove a vital factor in the curing of that awful disease.

DOUGLAS HURD

Douglas Hurd began his political life as a civil servant and looked destined to become one of Britain's ambassadors. This changed when he was appointed to head Edward Heath's office when the Conservatives were in opposition. When Mrs Thatcher was returned to power in 1979 she appointed him Minister of State at the Foreign Office. His first Cabinet appointment was that of Secretary of State for Northern Ireland, a post which he held for only a short time before becoming Home Secretary.

LADY WARNOCK

Lady Warnock is the Mistress of Girton College, Cambridge, and was created a Life Peer in 1985. A former Headmistress of Oxford High School, she is the author (with T. Devlin) of an intriguing book *What Must We Teach?* She must be the only Head of a Cambridge college who is married to the Head of an Oxford college, Geoffrey Warnock. Perhaps they meet from time to time going round one of those interminable roundabouts at Milton Keynes.

PROFESSOR ANNE BARTON

Professor Anne Barton was born and educated in the USA, but has made a distinguished academic career for herself in England, first at Oxford and since 1984 at Cambridge, where she is now a Fellow of Trinity College and Professor of English Literature. The author of important scholarly works on Shakespeare and Ben Jonson, Anne Barton has reached a wider audience of theatregoers through the entertaining essays she contributes to the programmes for the productions mounted by her director husband John Barton for the Royal Shakespeare Company.

MICHAEL CAINE

Michael Caine first came to prominence in 1966 for his superlative performance in the title role of *Alfie*. At the time some critics dismissed his performance as a one-off from a boy from the Old Kent Road who would not be heard from again. Since then he has been nominated for an Oscar on three occasions when acting alongside Laurence Olivier in *Sleuth*, Maggie Smith in *California Suite*, and in *Educating Rita* with Julie Walters. He has never hidden his disappointment at failing on these occasions, or his joy when he finally won an Oscar for his role in *Hannah and Her Sisters*.

TOYAH WILLCOX

Toyah Willcox, one of the wild girls of the 'punk rock' era, has proved to have a considerable performing talent in the spheres of singing and acting. She manages to combine a stream of top ten hits—some written by herself—with a varied film and theatrical career, including appearances opposite Katharine Hepburn and Laurence Olivier.

MICHAEL GAMBON

Michael Gambon is an actor's actor. Everyone who has seen him perform on the London stage knows they are in the presence of a consummate professional. He first came to prominence with the general public with his performance of the vet in Alan Ayckbourn's *Norman Conquests*. During the eighties he has dominated the National Theatre, winning almost every award the British stage has to offer.

— RICHARD EYRE —

Theatre, film and TV director Richard Eyre has been Associate Director of the National Theatre since 1981. Winner of several awards for directing in the eighties, there can be few theatregoers who have not seen a play directed by him in recent years—among them *The Beggar's Opera* and *The Government Inspector*. In 1988 he will succeed Sir Peter Hall as Director of the National Theatre.

PROFESSOR STEPHEN HAWKING

Despite the severe handicap of a wasting disease that leaves him crippled in a wheelchair and unable to talk without the aid of a voice synthesizer, Stephen Hawking has produced some of the most original and challenging work in the field of astro-physics since the beginning of the century. Lucasian Professor of Mathematics at Cambridge University, where he is also a Fellow of Gonville and Caius College, Stephen Hawking is the recipient of many honours, including the CBE (which he was awarded in 1982) and the Franklin Medal of the American Franklin Institute. He also has the reputation of being one of the wittiest men in the scientific community.

INDEX